How Sweet It Is

(and Was)

The History of Candy

by Ruth Freeman Swain

illustrated by John O'Brien

Holiday House
New York

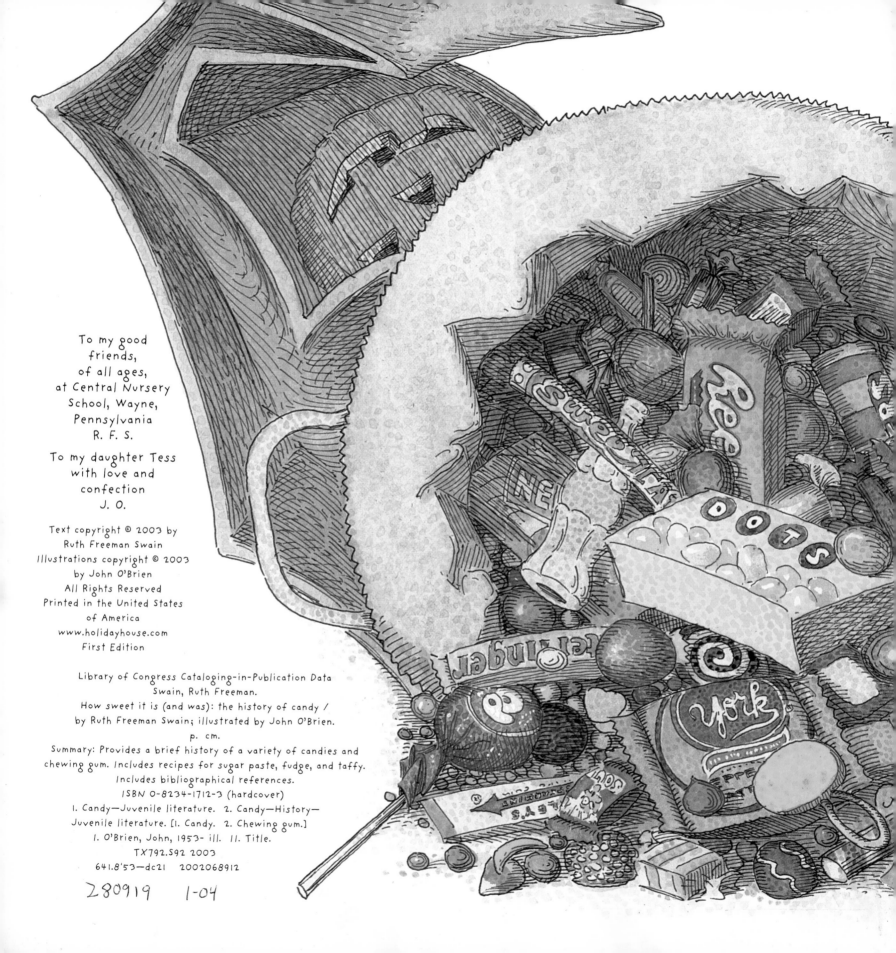

To my good
friends,
of all ages,
at Central Nursery
School, Wayne,
Pennsylvania
R. F. S.

To my daughter Tess
with love and
confection
J. O.

Text copyright © 2003 by
Ruth Freeman Swain
Illustrations copyright © 2003
by John O'Brien
All Rights Reserved
Printed in the United States
of America
www.holidayhouse.com
First Edition

Library of Congress Cataloging-in-Publication Data
Swain, Ruth Freeman.
How sweet it is (and was): the history of candy /
by Ruth Freeman Swain; illustrated by John O'Brien.
p. cm.
Summary: Provides a brief history of a variety of candies and
chewing gum. Includes recipes for sugar paste, fudge, and taffy.
Includes bibliographical references.
ISBN 0-8234-1712-3 (hardcover)
1. Candy—Juvenile literature. 2. Candy—History—
Juvenile literature. [1. Candy. 2. Chewing gum.]
I. O'Brien, John, 1953- ill. II. Title.
TX792.S92 2003
641.8'53—dc21   2002068912

Z80919   1-04

Is your favorite candy a creamy, crunchy chocolate bar, a piece of sour-apple bubble gum, or strawberry pebbles that explode in your mouth? How about the lime lollipop that looks like an emerald ring or lollipops that whistle or spin? Do you love licorice jelly beans, peanut brittle, hot cinnamon hearts, snappy peppermints, sticky caramels, or . . . all of the above?

Store shelves are filled with bright, shiny packages of candy in mouthwatering flavors and crazy, new shapes. Candy companies work hard to get you to buy their brand of candy. They keep their recipes locked in safes and are always looking for ideas for new kinds of candy. What will they come up with next?

Sometimes people want candy that's new and different, but sometimes they want the same kind of candy they've had before. What would Christmas be without candy canes, Valentine's Day without "conversation hearts," Hanukkah without chocolate coins, or a summer fair without cotton candy and lemon sticks? And can you imagine Halloween without candy?

The word "candy" comes from the Arabic *qandi*, which came all the way from the Indian Sanskrit word *khanda*, meaning a piece of sugar. India is where sugarcane was growing when people there first learned how to take the sweet juice from the tall canes.

Before sugar had come from the East, Egyptians, Greeks, and Romans made candy sweet with honey. Wall paintings show Egyptians keeping bees and making honey candies in molds.

Roman cities had shops where candy, or *dulcia*, was sold. "Dulcia" is the Latin word for "sweet." In one of the first cookbooks ever written, there is a Roman recipe for homemade *dulcia*: Dates are stuffed with chopped nuts and stewed in honey.

Sugar arrived in Europe during the Middle Ages with traders and knights returning from the Crusades. At first, only the richest people could afford sugar, even though they weren't quite sure what to do with it.

Some people thought sugar made a good medicine, like the sixteenth-century German doctor, Tabernaemontanus, who wrote, "Nice white sugar...cleans the blood, strengthens body and mind."

Many used it as a spice to add flavor or cover up tastes of rotten food. Then they discovered that sugar preserved fruits so they could be eaten later. This is how we got jams, jellies, and fruit leathers.

Maple sugaring has been a happy time for hundreds, maybe thousands, of years for people living in the northeastern United States. As the long winter ends and days grow warmer, maple trees are tapped to collect sap as it rises through the trunks to the branches.

Native Americans such as the Ojibwa in Minnesota and the Lenape in Pennsylvania discovered how to make maple syrup and maple sugar. They poured sap into bark pots and boiled it by adding sizzling rocks from a fire. Forty gallons of sap have to be boiled down to make one gallon of maple syrup. Then that gallon can be boiled longer to make three quarts of maple sugar.

Most of the maple sugar was kept to flavor breads and stews throughout the year. Some was stirred into water to make cool drinks on summer days. And some, while still hot, was poured onto the snow to make an icy, chewy treat.

English people living at the time of Queen Elizabeth I (1533–1603) and William Shakespeare (1564–1616) were crazy about "sweetmeats," as candy was called. "Dry suckets" were sugary lemon peels, "wet suckets" were fruits in syrups, and "kissing comfits" were small perfumed candies for sweetening people's breath. Queen Elizabeth kept her pockets filled with comfits and chewed so many her teeth turned black.

At royal banquets in the 16th and 17th centuries, huge sculptures made of sugar paste decorated the tables in great halls. A sugar paste ship, with flags and streamers flying, fired real gunpowder out of hollow plant stems at a gilded sugar castle. Unicorns and swans and lions and camels made of colored sugar paste all seemed to come to life. On one banquet table every platter and goblet was made out of sugar. When dinner was done, guests smashed their dishes and nibbled on them for dessert!

Chocolate comes from the warm, humid forests of Central America. Mayans and Aztecs learned how to roast the beans of the cacao tree, then grind and whip them with chili peppers and flowers. The spicy, frothy drink they made, *xocoatl*, was called the "food of the gods" and was drunk only by the king and members of his court.

Cacao beans were so valuable they were used for money: Four beans bought a pumpkin, ten bought a rabbit.

When the Spanish explorer Hernán Cortés (1485–1547) demanded to see the Aztecs' treasure, he was hoping for gold and spices. How could he know that the foaming, bitter-tasting drink he was given was one of the real treasures of this new world?

Cortés brought chocolate back to Spain, where it was kept a secret for almost a hundred years. But when a Spanish princess married King Louis XIV of France in 1659, the French, then all of Europe, fell in love with it.

During the late 17th century, "chocolate houses" in London served chocolate hot in tall, narrow cups. In France, fashionable ladies drank it at home with friends. Those chocolate drinks were no longer bitter and spicy; now they were sweetened with milk and sugar. By the late 17th century, sugar was widely available from the large sugar plantations in the West Indies, where many African slaves worked.

Country stores in 19th-century America sold "penny candy," candy that cost only a penny or two. There were jars of jelly beans, piles of peppermint sticks, boxes of lemon and molasses drops, trays of licorice and rock candy. Today the price sounds cheap, but in those days most children had very little money to spend and got candy only on special occasions.

Sometimes people made their own candy at home. On winter evenings, taffy-pulling parties were a chance for people to get together. Sugar and other ingredients were boiled to a high temperature, then cooled in pans. When it could be handled, the sticky taffy was pulled again and again between partners until it was soft and ready to be cut into pieces. It was fun as long as everyone remembered to grease his or her hands first. When Pennsylvania Germans made taffy, they called it "belly-guts" because the long, drooping strands of taffy looked like what hung in butcher shops!

Another homemade candy in late 19th-century America was a brand-new candy that began as a mistake. "Fudge" was a slang word for "mistake" and was probably discovered when a batch of caramels was "fudged," or ruined.

Fudge first became popular in 1888 when Emelyn Hartridge entered Vassar College and brought a little-known recipe with her that she'd gotten from a friend. When Emelyn cooked fudge over a gas lamp in her bedroom, her friends went nuts over it. Soon groups of girls were sneaking into each other's rooms after lights-out to whisper in the dark and stir up batches of fudge. The recipe spread to other women's colleges. Each one changed the recipe a bit, and fudge became even more popular.

Machines changed candy making in the early 20th century. Machines made candy faster, they made candies that always looked and tasted the same, and they made completely new kinds of candy, such as cotton candy.

In 1893 Milton Hershey (1857–1945) visited the Chicago Exposition, which was like a World's Fair, where he saw chocolate being made by European machines. He bought all the machines. He

worked hard to make a milk chocolate bar that everyone in America could afford. In 1900 he did it: His chocolate bar cost five cents. It was the first chocolate bar to be distributed across the country.

What are those wads on the sidewalk; those blobs on the bedpost, under your desk, or stuck in your hair? Chewing gum, bubble gum . . . Americans just love gum. But they weren't the first.

Early people chewed beeswax. Native Americans chewed spruce tree sap and shared the idea with the Pilgrims. Mayans chewed chicle, the gum or sap from the sapodilla tree. Chicle is very smooth and elastic.

In 1860, when General Santa Anna (1794–1876) was exiled from Mexico, he took some chicle with him to New York City. Years earlier, in 1836, he'd been a powerful military leader who defeated a small force of Texans at the Alamo. Now he was broke except for 250 kilos of chicle he hoped to sell as a rubber substitute.

Santa Anna never sold his chicle and, when he eventually returned to Mexico, he left it with his American friend Thomas Adams, who couldn't sell it either. One day Adams saw a little girl chewing wax and remembered how Santa Anna liked chewing bits of chicle. Adams began experimenting, boiling the chicle and adding flavors.

He introduced gumballs in 1871 and flat sticks of gum in 1875. They were a hit. The gum we chew today is made from synthetic chicle, but it's still a hit because chewing reduces stress, it helps relieve air pressure in our ears, and it's fun!

Candy has gone into space with astronauts, it's gone to war in field rations, it's been to the top of Mt. Everest. Candy is taken on car trips, camping trips, and backyard expeditions. It's eaten during movies and at baseball games and birthday parties.

Bite off a piece and chew. The taste is intense. It melts in your mouth, it tastes good, it feels good. It's an easy snack, a cheap treat; it fits in a hand or a pocket or right in your mouth. Mmm, how can you resist?

$C_{12} H_{22} O_{11}$ = SUGAR

The Facts—Short and Sweet

Candy's main ingredient is usually sugar or corn syrup, a sugar made from vegetables such as corn, but other sweeteners, such as molasses, honey, and fruit sugar, are sometimes used. Our bodies treat all sugars the same. Sugar gives us quick energy, but our bodies are able to produce sugar from starch. So sugar—and candy—are pure luxury foods. We don't need them at all.

So where does our "sweet tooth" come from? It may be because humans are born liking our first food, mother's milk, which is sweet. It may be because it was important for early people to eat sweet, ripe fruits, which are more digestible and better for us.

We taste sugar with the taste buds at the tip of our tongue. Our other taste buds detect sour, salty, and bitter tastes. Adults have about 10,000 taste buds on their tongues; children have even more, giving them a sharper sense of taste.

Sugar is just as bad for teeth as it's always been, but now researchers know that all refined carbohydrates can be a problem. This means that a piece of white bread can be as bad for your teeth as a candy bar. Taking good care of teeth is very important—especially if you want to enjoy your favorite candy for years to come.

Of course, some candies have fruits, grains, milk, and nuts, which are rich in nutrients. Chocolate has antioxidants, compounds that may help our bodies fight heart disease and certain cancers.

And what are some of those other ingredients on that candy label? Gums from various plants help thicken, or gel, the other ingredients. Carrageenan is a gum that comes from seaweed! Emulsifiers such as lecithin, which usually comes from soybeans, help two different ingredients blend together. Propylene glycol keeps moisture in food and helps certain flavors dissolve in water. Malic acid from apples, tartaric acid from grapes, and citric acid from lemons and limes are used for flavoring.

Whatever is in candy, we love to eat it—and eat it and eat it. Americans ate 7.1 billion pounds of candy in the year 2000. Each person, on average, ate almost twenty-five pounds of candy that year, more than twenty-six pounds if you add in gum. Chocolate is the most popular flavor. An average person eats almost twelve pounds of chocolate a year.

More candy is bought for Halloween than for any other holiday. In 2000 almost two billion dollars' worth of candy was sold at Halloween. But since statistics show that adults eat more candy than children, who was really eating the candy that night?

At least we don't eat as much candy per person as in some other countries. In the United Kingdom an average person eats thirty pounds of candy, or "sweets," a year, and in Denmark an average person eats thirty-six pounds!

Additional Information

Benning, Lee Edwards. *Oh, Fudge!* New York: Henry Holt and Company, 1990.

Cosman, Madeleine Pelner. *Fabulous Feasts: Medieval Cookery and Ceremony.* New York: George Braziller, 1976.

Simon, Charnan. *Milton Hershey: Chocolate King, Town Builder.* Chicago: Children's Press, 1998.

Tannahill, Reay. *Food in History.* New York: Crown Publishers, Inc., 1988.

Wardlaw, Lee. *Bubblemania: A Chewy History of Bubble Gum.* New York: Aladdin Paperbacks, 1997.

www.candyusa.org (website for the National Confectioners Association and the Chocolate Manufacturers Association)

Acknowledgments

Francie Owens at The Folger Shakespeare Library, Washington, D.C.

National Confectioners Association, McLean, VA

Goschenhoppen Historians, Inc., Vernfield, PA

Elizabeth Daniels and Nancy MacKechnie at Vassar College, Poughkeepsie, NY

Great Valley Nature Center, Devault, PA

Old Sturbridge Village, Sturbridge, MA

Mars, Inc., Hackettstown, NJ

Hershey Foods Corporation, Hershey, PA

Candy Time Line

1493	Columbus takes sugarcane seedlings to Americas on second voyage.
1502	Columbus is introduced to cacao on fourth and last voyage. Doesn't think much of it.
1519	Cortés drinks chocolate and brings recipe back to Spain. Chocolate and sugar continue to pass each other on the Atlantic for almost a hundred years before being combined.
1828	Dutch chocolate maker Conrad van Houten invents a cocoa press to extract cocoa butter and leave solid chocolate behind. Ground into a powder, cocoa can now be used in many more ways.
1848	"State of Maine Pure Spruce Gum" made in Bangor, Maine, out of spruce tree sap.
1866	Mottoes are first inscribed on pastel candy hearts for Valentine's Day by the Oliver R. Chase Company of Massachusetts.
1871	Thomas Adams introduces gumballs.
1875	In Switzerland Daniel Peter invents milk chocolate using Henri Nestlé's invention of condensed milk.
1875	Thomas Adams introduces flat sticks of gum.
1880s	Candy corn is created.

1893   Good & Plenty candy is made. It is the oldest brand-name candy still being sold in the U.S.

1896   Leo Hirshfield of New York makes Tootsie Rolls, naming them after his daughter's nickname, Tootsie.

1900   Milton S. Hershey distributes a five-cent milk chocolate bar.

1901   NECCO wafers appear, named for the acronym of the New England Confectionery Company.

1906   Hershey's Kisses chocolates appear in their foil wrappers.

1912   Life Savers—peppermint only—are sold. Fruit-flavored Life Savers won't appear for another 22 years.

1920   The Baby Ruth candy bar, named for President Grover Cleveland's daughter (not the baseball player), is sold.

1924   M&M Mars makes the Milky Way Bar.

1928	Walter Diemer, a 23-year-old accountant at the Fleer Chewing Gum Company, discovers a recipe for bubble gum. He makes it pink because that is the only color on hand.
1928	Reese's peanut butter cups, named for their inventor, are sold.
1929	M&M Mars makes the Snickers Bar, named for a racehorse owned by the Mars family.
1940–45	Hershey Chocolate Corporation makes 3 billion heat-resistant, high-energy chocolate bars for soldiers' field rations during World War II.
1940	M&M's plain chocolate candies are made.
1949	Smarties are introduced.
1949	250,000 packages of candy are dropped to children in blockaded Berlin during the Berlin Airlift.
1953	Sir Edmund Hillary and Tenzig Norgay are the first to climb Mt. Everest. They eat peppermints at the top.

1963	SweeTarts are introduced.
1971	Chocolate bars go to the moon with *Apollo 15* astronauts.
1974	Skittles are first sold.
1980	Gummy bears and gummy worms are made in America. Before this, they had been imported from Europe.
1998	Lollipops are sold with holograms printed on their surface.
1999	Radio lollipops are invented. Sound is transmitted from a radio lollipop holder, through the lollipop stick, and into your mouth. You hear the sound inside your head when you suck the lollipop!

Recipes

These recipes should be tried only with adult supervision. Precautions must be taken when sugar is heated to boiling temperatures because it is extremely hot.

Sugar Paste—16th to 17th centuries
(20th-century adaptation)

2 teaspoons lemon juice

4 teaspoons water

2 teaspoons (1 packet) unflavored gelatin, such as Knox gelatin

1 cup confectioners' sugar

extra confectioners' sugar as needed

Mix lemon juice, water, and gelatin in a bowl set in a larger bowl of hot water.

Stir until gelatin melts and loses its grainy appearance (this takes a few minutes).

Remove smaller bowl from larger bowl and knead in about a cup of confectioners' sugar.

Turn out onto a board dusted with confectioners' sugar.

With a rolling pin, roll out like pastry until sugar paste is $\frac{1}{8}$ to $\frac{1}{4}$ inch thick.

Use extra confectioners' sugar if needed, to avoid sticking.

Drape sugar paste over an upside-down plate or bowl.

Decorate edges if desired by cutting out shapes with a knife.

Let dry for a day or two in a cool, dry place until paste is firm and holds its shape.

Fill with candy or pieces of fresh fruit, and when that's eaten, you can eat the plate!

Vassar Fudge

2 ounces unsweetened chocolate, grated or smashed
2 cups granulated sugar
1 cup heavy cream
1 tablespoon cold butter
chopped nuts or pretzels (optional)

Children can have fun smashing the chocolate (in a plastic or paper bag) with a rolling pin on a hard surface.
Heat sugar, cream, and chocolate over low heat in a 2-quart saucepan till dissolved, while stirring occasionally.
Raise heat to medium and bring to a boil.
Continue to boil, stirring as little as possible, until a drop of chocolate placed in ice water keeps its shape and is slightly chewy.
(Don't be afraid to keep boiling the fudge. Wait until the ball of chocolate in ice water really is chewy and you can roll it in your fingers.)
Put saucepan in sink, add 1 tablespoon cold butter, don't stir, allow to cool (this takes a while).
When mixture is lukewarm and there is a skin on top, stir fudge thoroughly.
When it thickens and loses its sheen, add nuts or pretzels (optional).
Pour into greased 8-inch-by-8-inch pan and score with a knife.

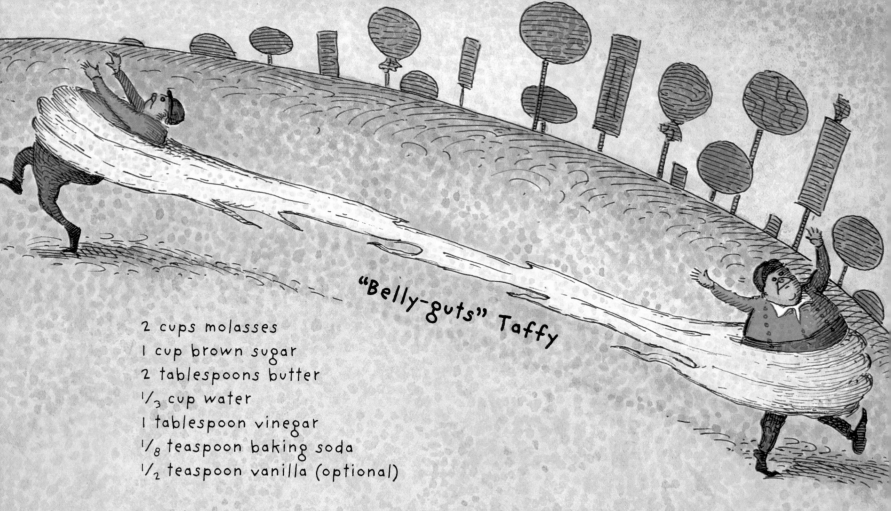

"Belly-guts" Taffy

2 cups molasses
1 cup brown sugar
2 tablespoons butter
1/3 cup water
1 tablespoon vinegar
1/8 teaspoon baking soda
1/2 teaspoon vanilla (optional)

In a large, heavy saucepan or pot with sides 4 to 5 inches high, cook molasses, brown sugar, butter, water, and vinegar, stirring constantly until sugar crystals are dissolved.

Continue cooking to 260°F (125°C) on a candy thermometer or until a small bit dropped in cold water forms a firm ball.

Add soda and vanilla, stir well, and pour into a well-greased shallow 8-inch-by-8-inch pan.

When cool enough to handle, butter or grease hands and pull candy into long ropes with a partner. Keep bringing it together and pulling it out again into long strands until it gets lighter in color. Cut into small pieces with scissors.